Doors

Drama by
SUZAN ZEDER

Dramatic Publishing Company
Woodstock, Illinois ● Australia ● New Zealand ● South Africa

*** NOTICE ***

The amateur and stock acting rights to this work are controlled exclusively by THE DRAMATIC PUBLISHING COMPANY, INC., without whose permission in writing no performance of it may be given. Royalty must be paid every time a play is performed whether or not it is presented for profit and whether or not admission is charged. A play is performed any time it is acted before an audience. Current royalty rates, applications and restrictions may be found at our website: www.dramaticpublishing.com, or we may be contacted by mail at: THE DRAMATIC PUBLISHING COMPANY, INC., 311 Washington St., Woodstock, IL 60098.

COPYRIGHT LAW GIVES THE AUTHOR OR THE AUTHOR'S AGENT THE EXCLUSIVE RIGHT TO MAKE COPIES. This law provides authors with a fair return for their creative efforts. Authors earn their living from the royalties they receive from book sales and from the performance of their work. Conscientious observance of copyright law is not only ethical, it encourages authors to continue their creative work. This work is fully protected by copyright. No alterations, deletions or substitutions may be made in the work without the prior written consent of the publisher. No part of this work may be reproduced or transmitted in any form or by any means, electronic or mechanical, including photocopy, recording, videotape, film, or any information storage and retrieval system, without permission in writing from the publisher. It may not be performed either by professionals or amateurs without payment of royalty. All rights, including, but not limited to, the professional, motion picture, radio, television, videotape, foreign language, tabloid, recitation, lecturing, publication and reading, are reserved.

> For performance of any songs, music and recordings mentioned in this play which are in copyright, the permission of the copyright owners must be obtained or other songs and recordings in the public domain substituted.

©1982 by SUZAN L. ZEDER
©1985 by ANCHORAGE PRESS INC.
© 2007 by SUZAN L. ZEDER

Printed in the United States of America
All Rights Reserved
(DOORS)

ISBN: 978-1-58342-933-4

IMPORTANT BILLING AND CREDIT REQUIREMENTS

All producers of the play *must* give credit to the author of the play in all programs distributed in connection with performances of the play and in all instances in which the title of the play appears for purposes of advertising, publicizing or otherwise exploiting the play and/or a production. The name of the author *must* also appear on a separate line, on which no other name appears, immediately following the title, and *must* appear in size of type not less than fifty percent (50%) the size of the title type. Biographical information on the author, if included in the playbook, may be used in all programs. *In all programs this notice must appear:*

"Produced by special arrangement with
THE DRAMATIC PUBLISHING COMPANY, INC., of Woodstock, Illinois."

DEDICATION

For, with, and because of Jim

A Note From the Playwright

This play began for me with a real child and a real divorce. A friend, whose marriage had recently exploded, shared a story about her ten year old son reaching out from his own pain and sadness to comfort her. It was an act of two human beings meeting in a moment of healing that went beyond the boundaries of a "social problem" into the realm of art. The story haunted me for years until I gave it a second life in the final lines of this play.

The next image that came to me was the door, and with it came the title. At first I didn't trust it. I thought the title needed to be something grander, more evocative. So I experimented with other titles such as Separate Doors, and Through Separate Doors. But the image was wiser than I, and the play must be called what it has always been, Doors.

The first production of this play in 1981 was its formative one. I am deeply grateful to Greg Falls for his initial commission and for the showcase production which gave the play its present substance and shape. Jim Hancock, my husband, was the director, but his role was that of a collaborator. This is as much his play as it is mine.

For fifteen years I have written plays about children, not from any social, educational, or therapeutic motivation, but simply because they fascinate me as a dramatist. I am profoundly interested in children as protagonists who find themselves in crises, who struggle against overpowering forces, and conduct themselves as heroes. I respect the efforts of parents and children facing troubled times with dignity and depth. I find these efforts to be legitimate and compelling dramatic territory.

I offer this play to you, not as an examination of a significant "social problem" but as a theatre experience which chronicles the journey of three individual survivors through a particularly difficult day.

Suzan Zeder
Dallas, Texas 1985

CHARACTERS

Jeff, eleven years old
Ben, his father
Helen, his mother
Sandy, his best friend

SETTING

Jeff's Room

TIME

The Present

DOORS was first commissioned by Gregory A. Falls and was showcased by A Contemporary Theatre at the Bush School in Seattle, Washington in 1981, with the following cast:

Jeff..Marco Sawrey
Ben.................................... William ter Kuile
Helen...............................Theresa DePaolo
Sandy.....................................Chris Devore

The production was directed by Jim Hancock

Production rights for this play are granted with the implicit understanding that it must be produced as written. With the exception of updating and localizing specific references, any cuts, changes, or alterations must be approved in advance and in writing by the publisher who will consult directly with the playwright.

DOORS
By Suzan L. Zeder

A fragmentary set suggesting Jeff's bedroom. At first glance it seems to be the rather ordinary room of an eleven year old boy; but there are odd angles, slanting doorways, and joints that do not quite connect. The whole room is slightly off kilter.

The room is dominated by a large closed door, center stage. It is the door to Jeff's parents' bedroom. Down left is a smaller door to the rest of the house. The walls of the room are defined by large scrimmed panels. The panels are decorated with posters of movies, mostly science fiction adventure films, currently popular at the time of the production. The posters are oversized and made of a scrim material; they are also hinged so that actors can pass through them.

Also in the room are a small bed, a couple of chairs, a desk or work area, a T.V. set, a stereo, and an over-flowing laundry basket.

At rise, JEFF is alone on stage, seated at the desk. He is working intently on a large, complicated model of a spaceship. The model is almost finished. JEFF works with great concentration with the directions and a tube of glue.

The first sounds we hear are muffled voices coming from Jeff's parents' room. They are arguing. This argument will be ongoing during most of the play; at times, specific voices and words will be heard, at other times, muffled sound, sometimes, nothing. Care should be taken to preserve the illusion that the argument is continuous without detracting from the primary focus which is to be on stage with Jeff and his actions. (See Production notes at the end of the script.)

JEFF tries to concentrate on his task of building the model, but he is obviously distracted and upset by the sounds coming from behind the door. He reads from the directions.

JEFF: 'When the glue is partially set, insert cockpit window flaps G and H into the main body of the craft.' *(The sounds of the argument grow louder and JEFF tries to concentrate harder.)* 'Hold firmly in place for a few seconds until the glue sets...' *(There is another sound from behind the door. JEFF looks up, the part slips. He tries again.)* 'When the glue is partially set, insert cockpit window flaps G and H into the main body of the craft.' (As JEFF lines up the parts, a series of angry bursts are heard, they register on his face, but he does not move.) ...

JEFF (Cont): 'until the glue sets' . . . *(JEFF rises, turns on the stereo set, and returns to the model)* 'Insert wheel hub N into wheel rim O and affix wheel assembly to landing gear C.' *(He looks all over the model.)* Where's the landing gear? Where's the landing gear? Where's that. . . (Sounds from behind the door increase. JEFF picks up the model, looking for the landing gear and the cockpit falls off. The phone rings. JEFF looks at the door. The phone rings again. JEFF tries to return to the model, the phone rings again.)* 'Insert wheel hub'. . yeah. yeah... yeah. . . 'affix to landing GEAR!' *(The phone continues to ring. Finally, JEFF rises and answers. The stereo is very loud.)*

Hello? Just a second. *(JEFF puts down the phone, crosses to the stereo and turns it off. He returns to the phone.)* Sorry. Hello, Gramma. Yeah, this is Jeff. Yeah, we got out of school last week... No, I'm not going to camp this year... Gramma, they don't have camps for Grandmothers. *(Sounds behind the door increase.)* Yeah, they're both here, but they can't come to the phone right now. They're in their room with the door closed and I don't think I'd better.... I'll tell them you called. I'm sure Mom will call you back later... Yeah, you too, Gramma. Bye. *(JEFF hangs up the phone, and crosses back to the desk, on the way he turns on the stereo and the T.V. very loud.)*
Stop it. Stop it! STOP IT!
(JEFF sits and buries his face in his hands; the sound is tremendous. After a beat, the large door bursts open and BEN enters angrily.)

BEN: Jeff! Turn it down! *(JEFF does not move.)* For Christ's sakes, Jeff! *(BEN crosses to T.V. and stereo and turns them off.)* We can't even hear ourselves think in there. Why does it have to be so loud?

JEFF: I like it loud.

BEN: Well, you're blasting us out of the house.

JEFF: Sorry.

BEN: Your Mother and I are trying to...talk and that doesn't help.

JEFF: Sorry.

BEN: If you're sorry, then keep it down. You can listen, but keep it reasonable, okay?
(BEN turns the stereo back on much lower and starts to exit back through the door. JEFF rises and stops him.)

JEFF: Hey, Dad?

BEN: *(Turning back to him)* Yeah?
(JEFF turns the stereo off)

JEFF: Gramma called.

BEN: Oh... What did she want?

JEFF: I don't know, just to talk I guess.

BEN: *(Under his breath, with frustration)* Oh, Brother...

JEFF: What?

BEN: Nothing. *(BEN notices that JEFF is really 'down'.)* Jeff? *(BEN, not sure of what do do, assumes a wrestling stance.)* Hey, Jeff?

JEFF: Oh, no, Dad! *(After a beat, JEFF responds with a wrestling stance. They mock wrestle, resulting in a much needed laugh for both of them.)*

HELEN: *(Spoken from off stage)* Ben?
(BEN starts to go, JEFF stops him.)

JEFF: Dad, can you have a look at this?

BEN: What?
(JEFF holds up the model.)

JEFF: The cockpit keeps falling off.

BEN: That's really coming along,

JEFF: Mom painted the flag and the wing trim.

BEN: I was going to help you with that. I'm sorry, Jeff.

JEFF: Mom helped me with the body and the engine.

BEN: But things kind of got away from me.

JEFF: I can't get the cockpit to stay on.

BEN: Let me see it. *(BEN inspects the model.)* Well, the flag is in the wrong place and the wing trim's crooked. But you put it together just fine.

JEFF: Really?

BEN: Oh, yeah. Have you got a razor blade? *(JEFF hands him a razor blade. BEN scrapes the glue.)* The surface has to be clean for it to seal. Now, the glue, *(BEN applies the glue and positions the cockpit.)*

JEFF: You've got to keep holding until the glue sets.

HELEN: *(OFF)* Ben?

BEN: In a minute!

JEFF: Look out, Dad, it's slipping.

BEN: I've got it.

JEFF: Your hands are shaking.

BEN: They are not!

JEFF: You've got to hold it still.

BEN: I know!
(There is a pause. BEN looks toward the door, back at JEFF, and toward the door again. JEFF notices.)

JEFF: Have a look at this. *(JEFF shows him an old photograph.)*

BEN: Where did you get that?

JEFF: I found it.

BEN: That's our old house on Beachcroft. What are you doing with that?

JEFF: I just like to look at it sometimes.

BEN: You remember that place?

JEFF: I remember.

BEN: But that was years ago.

JEFF: I remember.
(BEN takes the photo in one hand and holds the model in the other.)

BEN: I built every inch of that house. Built it and rebuilt it.

JEFF: I remember my bedroom; it had clouds and stars on the ceiling.

BEN: We painted them for you when you said that you wanted to sleep in the sky.

JEFF: When I turned out the lights, the stars glowed.

BEN: That was a good house, Jeff, a good house. Solid foundations, thick walls, none of that stucco, pre-fab garbage. I can't build 'em like that anymore.

JEFF: How come?

BEN: I haven't got the time, and who's got the money, and nobody cares.

JEFF: I miss that house.

BEN: Yeah, so do I. *(BEN puts down the photo and looks at JEFF.)* Jeff, there's something going on here, something we all have to talk about...

JEFF: *(Interrupting quickly)* Dad, you've got to hold on to it!

BEN: Huh?

JEFF: The cockpit, it's slipping again. You've got to hold it in place or it won't work.

BEN: I've got it.

JEFF: You've got to hold it steady.

BEN: I am holding it steady.
(HELEN enters and stands in the doorway.)

HELEN: What are you doing?

BEN: I'll be right there.

JEFF: Dad's helping me with my model.

HELEN: But, Ben...

BEN: I said, I'll be right there!

HELEN: Jeff, honey, you spend so much time inside these days, and it's a beautiful day out there. Why don't you go on over to Sandy's...

JEFF: I don't want to go to Sandy's.

HELEN: But, I thought you two were going to work on the movie.

JEFF: He's coming over here later.

HELEN: It's a beautiful day and here you are all cooped up.

BEN: He said, he didn't want to go.

HELEN: It was just a suggestion.

BEN: You know, you could have waited.

HELEN: Ben, I have been waiting...

BEN: I'm talking about this model.

HELEN: The model?

BEN: I was going to help him with it, just as soon as I got a little ahead on the Carlson development.

JEFF: It's okay, Dad.

HELEN: He needed help and he asked me.

BEN: You could have waited.

HELEN: Sure, I could have waited, but he couldn't.

JEFF: It's almost done now.

BEN: Just as soon as I finished the bids and worked out the contracts, and ....

HELEN: And when would that have been, Ben? Next week? Next month? Next year?

BEN: I was looking forward to it! (*The tension in their tone rises.*)

JEFF: *(Suddenly)* I don't feel well.

HELEN: *(Concerned)* What's the matter?

JEFF: I just don't feel so hot.

HELEN: Do you have a headache?

JEFF: I guess so.

BEN: He's all right.
(HELEN crosses to JEFF)

HELEN: Do you have a temperature?

JEFF: I don't think so.

BEN: He's all right.

HELEN: *(To Ben)* How do you know he's all right?

BEN: *(To Jeff)* You're all right, aren't you?

JEFF: I'm all right.

HELEN: But you just said...

BEN: He just said he was all right!

JEFF: Dad, the cockpit's all screwed up again.

BEN: Helen, will you let me finish this?

HELEN: I was just...

JEFF: The glue's all over the place. *(JEFF takes the model from BEN and returns to the desk with it.)*

HELEN: I'll be in our room when you're finished!
(HELEN exits through the large door and slams it as she goes.)

BEN: I'll be right there! *(BEN paces in anger as JEFF returns dejectedly to the model.)*

JEFF: Hand me the razor blade? *(BEN, distracted, does not answer.)* Dad, can you hand me the blade?

BEN: Oh, yeah, sure; just kind of scrape it there.... it'll be all right.

JEFF: Yeah.

BEN: Just hold it firm until the glue sets.

JEFF: Yeah.

BEN: You're all right aren't you?

JEFF: Yeah.
(BEN crosses to the large door, hesitates for a beat, then exits.)

HELEN: *(OFF)* When we discuss this with Jeff, will you at least do me the courtesy of allowing me to be there?

BEN: *(OFF)* We were talking about the model.

HELEN: *(OFF)* When we do talk to him, we can't be emotional and upset.

BEN: *(OFF)* I am NOT EMOTIONAL!

HELEN: *(OFF)* Then why are you shouting?

BEN: *(OFF)* I wasn't emotional then, now I'm emotional!
(JEFF slowly and deliberately pulls off the cockpit.)

HELEN: Stop shouting!

BEN: Stop picking! You always have to pick at me, at Jeff!
(JEFF breaks off one wing. BEN and HELEN continue off stage.)

HELEN: He said he didn't feel well.

BEN: He's all right.

HELEN: Just because you say he's all right, doesn't mean...

BEN: He said he was all right!
(JEFF snaps off the other wing.)

HELEN: I was just concerned!

BEN: Can't you leave anything alone?
(JEFF suddenly hurls the model at the door. It smashes onto

the floor and breaks into pieces. JEFF rises and turns both the stereo and the T.V. on full blast. He returns to his desk and cradles his head in his hands.)
(After a beat or so, SANDY is heard pounding on the smaller door.)

SANDY: *(OFF)* Jeff, you in there? Jeff? *(SANDY enters through the outside door. He lugs a life-sized dummy with him.)* Jeeze, Jeff, doesn't anyone around here answer the door? I've been out there about a half an hour ringing the bell and yelling. Hey, do you know the T.V. is on?
(JEFF pulls himself together, but avoids looking at SANDY.)

JEFF: Yeah.

SANDY: And the stereo, too? *(SANDY turns off the T.V.)* This much noise will rot your brain, at least that's what my Mom says.
(SANDY starts to turn off stereo.)

JEFF: Don't.

SANDY: Can I at least turn it down? *(JEFF looks toward the large door. SANDY turns it down but not off.)*

JEFF: What are you doing in here?

SANDY: I knew you were home and the front door was unlocked so I...

JEFF: What do you want?

SANDY: We've got to finish the script, remember?

JEFF: Look, Sandy, this isn't a good time.

SANDY: Don't you even want to see what I brought?

JEFF: What's that?
(SANDY holds up the dummy proudly.)

SANDY: It's a body for the crash scene! I figure we could put ketchup all over it for blood and maybe some dog food for brains.

JEFF: That's gross.

SANDY: Wait until you hear how I got it.

JEFF: Sandy... *(SANDY acts this out as he goes along.)*

SANDY: I was downtown in this alley behind Nordstroms and I saw this arm sticking out of a dumpster.... I thought some bum had crawled in there and died, but then I figured out that it was a dummy. So, I asked this big goon by the loading dock, if I could have it. And he said, 'It'll cost you a dollar.' So, I grabbed it and ran down Fifth like I was kidnapping it, or something. Then this number Fourteen bus came along, and I hopped on. The driver said, 'You can't bring that dummy on this bus!' So, I said, 'How dare you insult my brother!' And I paid two fares, sat it next to me, and talked to it all the way over here. Man, everyone on that bus really thought I was weird.

JEFF: You are weird. *(JEFF turns away.)*

SANDY: You're the weird one. I thought that would really crack you up. All the way over here, I just kept thinking, 'this will really crack Jeff up!' *(No response)* What's the matter?

JEFF: Nothing.

SANDY: Your report card! Your parents hit the ceiling about that F in science.

JEFF: I never showed it to them.

SANDY: The dog! You finally asked them if you could have a dog, and they said no, and...

JEFF: I haven't asked them about that yet.

SANDY: Then what's wrong?
(Sounds can be heard from behind the door.)

JEFF: Sandy, I'll come over to your house later and...

SANDY: Did you get the video camera from your dad?

JEFF: Uhhhh, he's been out of town.

SANDY: You mean you haven't even asked him yet?

JEFF: I'll ask him.

SANDY: We've got to start shooting tomorrow!

JEFF: I'll ask him later.

SANDY: Alright! How's the star ship coming along?

JEFF: *(Pointing towards the door)* It's over there.
(SANDY crosses to the door and picks up the wrecked model.)

SANDY: What happened to the star ship?

JEFF: It got hit by a meteor shower!

SANDY: It got hit by something! Jeff, the wings are all broken and the frame is cracked! These things cost a lot of money!

JEFF: I'll pay you back! I'll buy you another one! What more do you want?

SANDY: Jeff, we are supposed to be doing this together and all you're doing is screwing up!
(More sounds are heard)

JEFF: I don't want to do this today! Go home, Sandy. I'll call you later.

SANDY: I'm not leaving until we finish the script! And I'm turning that thing off! *(SANDY switches off the stereo; for a second the sounds of the argument can be heard, SANDY hears it and chooses to ignore it. JEFF turns away. SANDY pulls some pages out of his pocket.)* Okay, we start with a long shot of the ship hurtling toward the death asteroid. Then we show the crash... This will work great! *(He sarcastically holds the model up.)* Then we show the crew, those who haven't been burned alive or had their heads split open. . . *(He indicates the dummy.)* . . . struggling out of the wreck. *(SANDY acts this out as he goes along; JEFF watches, becoming more and more involved.)* Colonel McCabe is the first one out; that's me. Then comes Rocco, the navigator; that's Paul; and then the ship's doctor, old blood and guts; that's Rick; and finally comes the ship's robot computer, C.B. 430; that's you...
(JEFF suddenly joins in.)

JEFF: Suddenly, the robot computer starts acting strangely. His lights flash and smoke comes out of his ears. He walks toward the ship's doctor and grabs him... *(JEFF grabs the dummy.)* He punches him in the stomach, hits him in the head, crushes him in his steel grip and throws his lifeless body to the ground. *(JEFF beats-up the dummy and throws it.)*

SANDY: *(Laughing)* Rick's not going to like that.

JEFF: Then he whirls around and walks toward Rocco.

(JEFF turns in a circle and grabs the dummy again.) He grabs him by the arms and twists them out of their sockets! He throws him on the ground, time after time, after time, after time. *(JEFF slams the dummy on the floor.)*

SANDY: Jeff?

JEFF: *(Totally carried away)* He kicks him in the stomach, in the back, in the head, in the guts!

SANDY: Jeff, that's not in the script.

JEFF: Finally, he turns on Colonel McCabe. *(JEFF turns on him and stalks him.)*

SANDY: Cut it out, Jeff.

JEFF: Coming at him, slowly, slowly...

SANDY: I said, cut it out.

JEFF: Closer and closer. *(JEFF moves in and SANDY grows alarmed.)*

SANDY: Stop it!

JEFF: He raises his arm...

SANDY: Jeff! *(JEFF backs him up until he is next to the bed.)*

JEFF: And zap! The death ray! Colonel McCabe collapses in agony.
(SANDY is forced down on the bed. He is angry and confused.)

SANDY: He does not.

JEFF: He does too.

SANDY: Colonel McCabe does not die! It says in the script, I don't die!

JEFF: You will if I want you to.

SANDY: I will not!

JEFF: Who's got the camera?

SANDY: I don't know, Jeff. Who does? *(JEFF turns away.)* You're such a jerk! I'm going home!

JEFF: Get out of here!

SANDY: I am!

JEFF: And take this piece of junk with you! *(JEFF throws the dummy at SANDY.)* Go home to your Mommy and your Daddy, clear out of here and leave me alone!

SANDY: You're a stupid jerk, Jeff. You've been acting like a stupid jerk ever since your parents first started...

JEFF: You shut up about my parents! You don't know anything about my parents!

SANDY: I know that they're yelling again. Jeff, I've heard them ever since I've been here. I could even hear them down on the street.

JEFF: Get out of here, Sandy!

SANDY: I know all about it. *(JEFF turns away.)* My Mom told me. Your Mom talks to my Mom; they gab all the time.

JEFF: *(Without turning to him)* What did she say?

SANDY: She said that there was trouble over here and I should keep my big nose out of it. *(JEFF sits, upset. SANDY hesitates and approaches cautiously.)* You want to talk about it in the pact?

JEFF: The pact?

SANDY: You remember the pact, Jeff?

JEFF: We were just little kids.

SANDY: You remember how we both pissed on that dead frog and buried it? How we both cut our fingers and spit and swore with our blood that we would always tell each other everything?

JEFF: We were just little kids.

SANDY: Yeah.

JEFF: *(After a pause)* I don't care anymore, Sandy. They can scream at each other until they're hoarse, I don't care. They can slap each other around all day, I don't care. I just want it to stop.

SANDY: Do they really hit each other?

JEFF: I don't know. I don't care!

SANDY: Jeeze, I don't know what I'd do if my parents ever hit each other.

JEFF: I didn't say they did. I just said, I didn't care.

SANDY: Do you ever see them?

JEFF: I never see anything, it's always behind the door.

SANDY: Do they ever come down for breakfast in the morning, you know, with black eyes or bruises?

JEFF: Blow it out your ear, Sandy!

SANDY: Do you know what it's about?

JEFF: Nobody tells me anything.

SANDY: Do you know when it started?

JEFF: I knew something was up when they started having all these appointments. When I'd ask Mom where she was going, she'd say, 'Your Father and I have an appointment.'
(Lights change and we see BEN and HELEN. The following scene is played as though they are each speaking to an off stage counselor. The boys continue with their dialogue, seemingly oblivious to the words of BEN and HELEN.)

BEN: It all started about two years ago, Doctor. She went back to college for her Master's degree.

HELEN: It all started about four years ago. He stopped building houses and started building condominiums.

JEFF: *(To SANDY)* But it really started last Tuesday. Dad left and was gone for two days. Mom told me he was on a business trip, but he wasn't.

HELEN: 'Condominiums', he said, 'that's where the money is!' But the time? Time for electricians, carpenters, and clients; no time for us. So, I went back to school.

BEN: A Master's degree in Psychology? Why didn't she study something useful?

JEFF: When he came back, they tried to pretend everything was all right. But everything had changed.

HELEN: I changed. I discovered I have my own ideas, feelings, needs...

BEN: I need her to be with me while I'm building something for all of us.

JEFF: Now, everything's different.

SANDY: But do you know why?

BEN: I don't know why. She talks to me now, I don't understand what she's saying. She tells me I'm not giving her enough.

HELEN: When Ben gives, he gives things. When I give, I give things up.

JEFF: Something's happened, Sandy, I'm afraid it's something big.

HELEN: I won't give this up! It's my one chance to make something of my own.

BEN: I can't start all over again. This isn't just a job, it's my life!

JEFF: They hardly ever look at each other.

SANDY: Yeah?

BEN: We're tearing each other apart.

JEFF: They almost never talk to each other.

SANDY: Yeah?

HELEN: I want to put it back together again, with all the same pieces, but I want them to fit together differently.

JEFF: And they never ever smile at each other.

BEN: I want out: *(Lights out behind the posters. They appear to be solid again.)*

SANDY: Jeeze.

JEFF: Every night, when they think I'm asleep, Dad gets in his car and leaves. By morning he's back at the breakfast table.

Every morning we eat breakfast in silence.
(BEN and HELEN enter in fantasy. HELEN carries a tray of utensils which transforms JEFF'S desk into a breakfast table. The scene is played with tension and counterpuntal rhythms. JEFF sits at the middle of the table. HELEN stirs a pot of hot cereal. BEN enters. She stops. They glare at each other. HELEN continues to stir as BEN pours coffee, sits, and opens a newspaper. HELEN stirs in an ever increasing rhythm. BEN ignores her. Finally, she crosses to him, stirs faster and faster and dumps a spoonful into his bowl. BEN looks at her and then at the bowl. JEFF doggedly eats his cereal, scraping the bowl. HELEN pours herself a cup of coffee, and stirs it with her spoon clinking on the cup. BEN shoots her a look and retreats to his paper. JEFF eats and retreats to a comic book. HELEN speaks to JEFF but looks at BEN.)

HELEN: Don't read at the table, Jeff! It's rude. *(BEN crumples his paper. JEFF begins to tap his foot in a habitual nervous gesture. HELEN taps her foot in a similar rhythm. BEN speaks to JEFF, but looks at HELEN.)*

BEN: Don't tap your foot, son. It's very annoying.
(HELEN glares at BEN. BEN picks up a piece of toast and scrapes it into his cereal bowl. JEFF eats, noticing everything, but pretending to see nothing.)

BEN: *(meaning the opposite)* Don't you just LOVE cream of wheat, Jeff?
(HELEN rises and clears the table, and exits leaving BEN with the spoon twirling in the air. BEN rises and leaves the table. JEFF beats his hand down on the table as the lights return to normal.)

JEFF: I hate breakfast.

SANDY: Maybe you shouldn't have read at the table.

JEFF: It wouldn't have made any difference.

SANDY: My parents do that kind of thing all the time. It's like they have a secret code or something; they don't even have to talk, they read each other's minds.

JEFF: It used to be that way with my folks too; but now it's like they are screaming at each other, but their voices are so high pitched that only dogs can hear them.

SANDY: Jeeze.

(Voices can be heard from behind the door. JEFF turns away. SANDY is a bit curious.)

SANDY: Jeff, do you ever, you know, listen?

JEFF: Huh?

SANDY: I mean, when they fight, do you, you know, try to hear what they're saying?

JEFF: Sandy, I spend most of my time trying not to hear.

SANDY: Well, sometimes my folks argue, they don't really fight or anything; but when they argue, part of me tries to shut it out and part of me really wants to know what's going on.

JEFF: *(Not unkindly)* You little creep!

SANDY: No, but the weird thing is, the really weird thing is, whenever I listen, it all sounds so stupid! Like last year, you know, we all went down to Puyallup, to the fair. We go every year, and every year the same thing happens. *(SANDY uses a couple of chairs to setup a 'car' and he plays out the following.)*
My Dad always drives and my Mom sits next to him and does needlepoint. Julie, Carrie, and I sit in the back seat and argue over who has to sit on the hump. After we have been driving for about a half an hour, my Mom looks up and says, 'We always go this way and we always get lost.'
Then my Dad says, 'You got a better route?'
And my Mom says, 'Back there at the service station, I told you to turn left.'
'But that's the way all the traffic goes.'
'That's because it's the right way.'
'There's less traffic this way.'
'THAT'S because we're going to Auburn'.
Then, Julie says, 'But I thought we were going to the fair!'
And they both say, 'Be quiet, Julie.'
And my Mom says, 'Daddy's trying to drive.'
And Dad says, 'What's that supposed to mean?'
So, my Mom says, 'It's not supposed to mean anything. I am just trying to get us to the fair. If you'd listen instead of charging ahead, we wouldn't be lost.'
Then, Dad says, 'Who's lost? I know exactly where we are.'
And Mom says, 'Okay, where are we?'
And we all say, 'WE'RE LOST!' Then they both turn around and yell at US.

JEFF: Did you get to the fair?

SANDY: Yeah.

JEFF: How was it?

SANDY: It was great.

JEFF: With my folks we'd never get there. *(JEFF takes SANDY'S place and acts out the following)*

JEFF: My Mom would say, 'The reason you're driving this way is because you really don't want to go to the fair.'
And my Dad would say, 'What?'
'You didn't want to go last night when I suggested it and you didn't want to go this morning, while I was packing the picnic. That's why you didn't help.'
'You said, you didn't need any help.'
'Still, it would have been nice.'
'Nice? I'm being nice. I'm taking you to the fair aren't I?'
'Only because you feel guilty.'
'Guilty?'
'Because you didn't take us last year.'
'But I'm taking you this year! I am taking you to the god-damned fair when I should be at the office.'
'See, I knew you didn't want to go.'
Then we'd turn around and all the way back to Seattle all you'd hear would be the sound of ice melting in the cooler.

SANDY: Did that really happen?

JEFF: No, but that's what would have happened.

SANDY: How do you know.?

JEFF: I know, believe me, I know.

SANDY: What do you know?

JEFF: I know that's what would have happened.

SANDY: That's not what I mean. What do you know about what's happening?

JEFF: I don't know.

SANDY: You don't know what you know?

JEFF: No! What are you talking about?

SANDY: Look Jeff, if you can figure out what's going on, then maybe you can do something about it.

JEFF: I've tried.

SANDY: Well, try again! What are the facts?

JEFF: You sound like something out of C.S.I. *(Update to any popular police or detective show.)*

SANDY: I'm just trying to help. *(SANDY leaps to his feet and becomes a detective.)* Come on, man, what do you know?

JEFF: I know my Dad's not sleeping at home at night.

SANDY: Okay, where does he go?

JEFF: I don't know.

SANDY: Well, if he's not sleeping at home, he has to be sleeping somewhere else.

JEFF: Brilliant.

SANDY: Have you asked him?

JEFF: No.

SANDY: Why not?

JEFF: I can really see me going up to my father and saying, 'Where you been sleeping these days, Dad?' Get real.

SANDY: We may have to tail him.

JEFF: I'm not going to do that!

SANDY: It was just a suggestion. Say, Jeff, do you think he's got a ... girlfriend.

JEFF: No.

SANDY: Why not?

JEFF: He just wouldn't!

SANDY: Okay, scratch that. What else do you know?

JEFF: I know they fight a lot.

SANDY: What about?

JEFF: Everything.... Anything.

SANDY: You must have heard something in particular.

JEFF: This afternoon, I heard my Mom say, 'I'm not giving up.'

SANDY: Giving up what?

JEFF: I couldn't hear.

SANDY: Smoking! Your Dad wants her to give up smoking!

JEFF: She doesn't smoke.

SANDY: When my Mom tried to give up smoking, she threw a whole plate of spaghetti at my Dad. She said it slipped, but I knew she threw it.

JEFF: I said, she doesn't smoke.

SANDY: You sure?

JEFF: She's my Mother!

SANDY: What else did you hear?

JEFF: I heard my Mom say something about a job.

SANDY: YOUR DAD LOST HIS JOB!

JEFF: I don't think...

SANDY: That's it! Jeff, I saw this thing on 'Sixty Minutes,' about how all these people are losing jobs. First they lose the job, then they go on welfare, then everybody starts fighting with everybody and...

JEFF: My Dad works for himself, he's a contractor.

SANDY: Oh no, Jeff! That's the worst.

JEFF: Do you really think....

SANDY: Here, I'll show you. *(SANDY grabs the dummy and mimes the characters with it.)* Here is your Father, sitting around reading his paper. And your Mother comes in and says, 'Well, I certainly hope that you're looking for a job.' And he says, 'Job,

I have a job.' And she says, 'I mean a job with some money!' 'Maybe if you wouldn't spend so much on cigarettes and panty hose...'

JEFF: I told you, she doesn't...

SANDY: And she says, 'Me spend so much? You're such a cheapskate.

JEFF: Sandy...

SANDY: And that really makes him mad so he hauls off and... Bam! SLAM! POW! THWACK! *(SANDY makes the dummy punch the air. JEFF grabs it from him.)*

JEFF: I never said they hit each other!

SANDY: I was just trying to...

JEFF: I've never seen them hit each other. They're not like that at all! *(Pause.)*

SANDY: Hey, Jeff, why don't you just ask them what's going on? *(JEFF tenderly carries the dummy over to the bed.)* Ask your Mom, she'll tell you something. My mother always tells me something.

JEFF: I just want it to stop, Sandy. Every night when I hear them in there, I put the pillow over my head, so I can't hear them and I try to imagine what it would be like if they would just stop fighting. I try to make myself dream about it. If they would just stop fighting, everything would be perfect. *(JEFF covers the dummy's head with a pillow during this speech. Lights change and there is music as we move into his fantasy.)* It would be morning; and the first thing I hear would be Mom, in the kitchen making breakfast. The first thing I smell would be bacon frying. The first thing I feel would be sunlight on my face.

(LIGHTS come up on HELEN.)

HELEN: Jeff, time to get up! Time for breakfast!

JEFF: So, I'd get up, and I'd come downstairs.
(JEFF manipulates the dummy out of bed, and brings it to the desk which will serve once again as a breakfast table. HELEN enters with utensils. JEFF enters the scene with the dummy. He manipulates the dummy and all relate to it as though it were him.)

HELEN: Morning.

JEFF: Morning.

HELEN: Sleep well?

JEFF: Very. *(JEFF seats the dummy at his place.)*

HELEN: Ben, breakfast is ready.

BEN: I'll be right there. *(BEN enters the scene. He takes his place at the table. Everything is warm and loving, unreal and exaggerated.)*

HELEN: Morning.

BEN: Morning.

HELEN: Sleep well?

BEN: Very.
(HELEN hands BEN a plate with obvious pleasure.)

BEN: *(Delighted)* Eggs over easy, hash browns, bacon, toast, coffee with cream and two sugars. Thank you, dear.

HELEN: You're welcome, darling.

BEN: *(To the dummy)* Morning, son.

JEFF: *(Nodding the dummy toward BEN.)* Morning.

BEN: Sleep well?

JEFF: Very.
(HELEN sits at table and all mime eating.)

JEFF: *(To SANDY)* In this family everyone eats breakfast.

HELEN: This afternoon, I thought we'd all go to the circus. I've called for the tickets. They're at the box office.

BEN: This afternoon, I thought we'd all go to the Sonics game. I've called for the tickets, they're at the box office.

HELEN: But, Dearest, the circus ...

BEN: But, Darling, the Sonics ...

HELEN: Circus.

BEN: Sonics. *(Tension begins to build)*

HELEN: CIRCUS!

BEN: SONICS!

JEFF: In this family there is NEVER any arguing.

HELEN: We'll go to the Sonics!

BEN: We'll go to the Circus!

JEFF: In this family there is ALWAYS a solution.

SANDY: In this family there is a dog!
(SANDY enters the scene as a boisterous slobbering dog. He bounds around the room.)

HELEN: Who let the dog in?

BEN: He's all right! Here, Boy! Atta Boy! Good Dog. Good Boy!

HELEN: *(Pleasantly)* Ben don't you think he should really be outside?
(SANDY bounds playfully over to BEN, jumps on him and they tussle.)

BEN: Hey, Jeff, have a look at this. Fetch, boy. *(BEN throws an imaginary object and SANDY bounces after it.)*

HELEN: Please, Ben, not in the house.

JEFF: Sandy!

BEN: Good dog! Bring it here. Good boy!
(SANDY fetches it and knocks into the table.)

HELEN: Ben, he's knocking over the table.

BEN: Oh, he's just a puppy.

JEFF: Sandy... *(BEN throws the object again.)*

BEN: After it, boy!
(SANDY leaps onto the bed and kicks up the covers.)

HELEN: He's tearing up the house. Stop it, Ben.

JEFF: Stop it, Sandy.
(SANDY knocks over the hamper, scattering the contents.)

HELEN: *(Very angry)* Ben, that dog just made a mess on the living room carpet!

BEN: Don't yell at me, I didn't do it!

JEFF: Stop, it, Sandy!

HELEN: He's tearing up my house.

BEN: Your house? I thought this was my house, too!

HELEN: Well, if it's your house, then you can clean it up! *(HELEN exits.)*

BEN: I'll have MY dog in MY house any damn time I want! *(BEN exits. The lights return to normal.)*

JEFF: You spoiled everything! There aren't any dogs in this house!
(JEFF kicks SANDY who yelps like a dog, and dives under the bed.)

SANDY: You kicked me!

JEFF: Why did you do that?

SANDY: I was just fooling around and you kicked me.

JEFF: Come out of there.

SANDY: Not until you say you're sorry.

JEFF: I'm sorry.

SANDY: You don't really mean it.

JEFF: I said I was sorry.

SANDY: Get down on your knees and say it.
(JEFF gets down on his knees, reluctantly.)

JEFF: I'm sorry, I'm sorry, I'm sorry! Now, come on out!
(Just as SANDY starts out, the large door opens and HELEN enters in reality. SANDY ducks back under the bed.)

HELEN: Jeff!

JEFF: *(Startled)* Huh?

HELEN: What are you doing?

JEFF: Nothing.

HELEN: What happened to your room?

JEFF: I'll clean it up.

HELEN: Never mind about that now, I didn't come in to talk about your room. Your Dad and I need to talk to you.

JEFF: What about?

HELEN: About all of us.

JEFF: Why?

HELEN: Just come on in. I think we'll be more comfortable in there. *(HELEN indicates their room, JEFF pulls away.)*

JEFF: I'm cleaning my room.

HELEN: That can wait.

JEFF: I'm busy.

HELEN: Jeff, we need to talk to you now.

JEFF: I just want you to leave me alone.

HELEN: We've left you alone too much, but now we need to talk. Daddy's waiting... *(JEFF pulls away and kicks the remains of the model which has wound up on the floor.)* Your model? What happened to your model? *(HELEN picks up the smashed model.)*

JEFF: I broke it.

HELEN: How?

JEFF: I just did. I smashed it.

HELEN: But you were so careful.

JEFF: I made it and I can smash it if I want! *(JEFF lunges for it and HELEN holds it out of his grasp.)*

HELEN: Not after we worked so hard on it.

JEFF: What do you care?

HELEN: I care.

JEFF: *(Explodes)* Oh yeah, you care a lot, a whole damn lot! *(HELEN, exhausted, sits on his bed.)*

HELEN: I am so tired of fighting, Jeff. I don't want to fight with you.

JEFF: Then don't. Just go away and leave me alone!

HELEN: Jeff, do me a favor. Just sit here with me for one minute and let's not talk, let's not even think.

JEFF: Why?

HELEN: Please.
(JEFF sits, sullen at first: HELEN sighs. After a few seconds, HELEN starts to say something; JEFF catches her eye and looks at his watch; she is silent. HELEN reaches out to him and he slides closer to her. They relax in a moment of mutual comfort. In the silence, JEFF's anger is defused, for the moment. HELEN holds him and her face betrays her sorrow, pain, and concern. After a beat, JEFF speaks.).

JEFF: Are we on welfare?

HELEN: What?

JEFF: Did Dad lose his job?

HELEN: No. What ever gave you that idea?

JEFF: Just something I heard.

HELEN: Heard? Heard where?

JEFF: *(Nods toward the large door)* I heard you guys yelling something about a job.

HELEN: Oh, Jeff, I'm sorry; I didn't want you to hear about it like that. I wanted to tell you myself as soon as I was sure.

JEFF: Tell me what?

HELEN: I've been offered a job with a Community Mental Health Center in Portland.

JEFF: Portland?

HELEN: It's a good job, a very good job, and it could be important to both of us.

JEFF: You aren't going to take it, are you?

HELEN: I haven't decided yet.

JEFF: So that's what it's all about, I mean with you and Dad.

HELEN: What's happening with us has very little to do with this job.

JEFF: You have to tell them no.

HELEN: If I thought that would solve anything, I would. Your Dad and I have problems, serious ones. They don't need to be your problems, but they do affect you, so we need to talk.

JEFF: I don't want to talk, anymore.

HELEN: If you would rather talk here, I'll go get your Dad and...
  (HELEN starts out.)

JEFF: Why don't you get a job here?

HELEN: That wouldn't help.

JEFF: You could find a job here!

HELEN: That wouldn't change anything.

JEFF: There must be all sorts of jobs here that you could...

HELEN: IT'S NOT THE JOB!

JEFF: I don't want to talk to you.

HELEN: Jeff. . . *(JEFF turns away.)*

JEFF: I won't listen to anything you say!

HELEN: Stop it! *(JEFF claps his hands over his ears.)*

JEFF: I can't hear you.

HELEN: I want you to stop this right now! *(SANDY sneaks out from under the bed and tries to slip out the door. HELEN catches sight of him.)* Sandy!

SANDY: *(Embarrassed)* Excuse me.

HELEN: I didn't know anyone was here.

JEFF: I said, I was busy.

SANDY: I uhhhhhhh, gotta be going.

HELEN: *(To JEFF)* Why didn't you tell me?

SANDY: I'm sorry, Mrs. Stuart.

HELEN: Sandy, Jeff's Dad and I need to talk to him.

SANDY: Yeah, I know.

HELEN: I think you had better....

SANDY: I'm going right now, Mrs. Stuart.

JEFF: Can I at least say good bye to him?

HELEN: Yes.

JEFF: Alone?

HELEN: Come into our room when you're done. Good bye, Sandy.

SANDY: Bye, Mrs. Stuart. Uhhhh, Mrs. Stuart?

HELEN: Yes?

SANDY: I didn't mean to listen. I didn't hear much.

HELEN: Good bye, Sandy. Say hello to your Mother for me. We'll be waiting, Jeff.

JEFF: I'll come when I'm ready.

(HELEN exits through the large door. SANDY picks up the dummy and starts toward the small door.)

SANDY: Bye, Jeff. See you tomorrow.

JEFF: Don't go.

SANDY: You heard what she said.

JEFF: Don't go!

SANDY: But, Jeff...

JEFF: Please, Sandy, just for a little while.

SANDY: They're waiting for you.

JEFF: I know.

SANDY: I feel weird.

JEFF: I'll go in there when I'm ready, not right now.
(SANDY sits and looks at JEFF. There is an awkward moment between them. SANDY looks at the door and then at his watch.)

SANDY: When do you think you'll be ready, Jeff?

JEFF: Something's got to happen. Something big, something so she won't take that job.

SANDY: Didn't you listen? She said it wasn't the job.

JEFF: Something to make them stop fighting.

SANDY: Like what?

JEFF: Like if something happened to me. Like if I got hit by a truck or something.
(JEFF jumps up, makes a wailing sound, grabs the dummy and runs around the room. He dumps the dummy face down on the desk and lights begin a gradual change as he moves into fantasy. SANDY does not join the fantasy as quickly.)

SANDY: Jeff?

JEFF: Doctor, we have a very serious case here, a very serious case.

SANDY: Jeff...

JEFF: I said, Doctor we have a serious case here, a very serious case.

SANDY: I gotta go home.

JEFF: Please, Sandy! We have a serious case here. *(SANDY reluctantly crosses to the desk, which has become an operating table, and joins in.)*

SANDY: Name?

JEFF: Jeff Stuart.

SANDY: Age?

JEFF: Eleven.

SANDY: Pulse?

JEFF: Weak!

SANDY: Heartbeat?
(JEFF listens at the dummy's chest.)

JEFF: Going, going, GONE!

SANDY: EMERGENCY! *(Both boys pound frantically on the dummy's chest.)* Hold it!

JEFF: What is it?

SANDY: It's started again. He's better now. *(SANDY tries to leave the fantasy, JEFF pulls him back.)*

JEFF: No, we have to operate!

SANDY: Operate?

JEFF: OPERATE! Knife! *(JEFF holds up an imaginary knife SANDY assumes the role of the Doctor. JEFF slaps the knife into his hand.)*

SANDY: Knife! *(SANDY mimes the operation, JEFF makes sound effects. SANDY opens the 'patient'.)* Oh, gross!

JEFF: Look at his guts.

SANDY: All twisted up.

JEFF: Look at his liver.

SANDY: That's disgusting.

JEFF: He's losing a lot of blood!

SANDY: TRANSFUSION! *(SANDY stands with one arm raised and his hand cupped, like a plasma bottle. JEFF jabs SANDY'S other arm at the dummy's arm.)* Glub, glub, glub... *(SANDY slowly closes his hand as though the bottle were emptying.)* We saved him again; he's better now! *(SANDY tries again to leave the fantasy; JEFF won't let him.)*

JEFF: No! The parents have to be notified.

SANDY: *(Dropping the fantasy)* Jeff, this isn't going to help.

JEFF: Sandy, we have got to call the parents! *(JEFF crosses to the phone, picks up the receiver and hands it to SANDY)* Tell them to come right away! *(JEFF makes SANDY take it.)* Ring! Ring!
(Lights come up on BEN and HELEN each holding a phone receiver.)

BEN and **HELEN**: Hello.

JEFF: *(To SANDY)* Tell them!

SANDY: This is the hospital! We have your son here. You'd better come right away.

BEN and **HELEN**: Oh, my God!
(BEN and HELEN enter the scene. They each take a chair and establish a waiting room. JEFF crosses to them, SANDY hangs back and watches.)

JEFF: Mr. and Mrs. Stuart?

HELEN: Is he going to be all right?

JEFF: Too soon to tell.

BEN: Is he going to make it?

JEFF: That all depends.

BEN and **HELEN:** On what?

JEFF: On what you do now. We've done everything that medical science can do for him. Now, you take him home and take good care of him. He needs rest and peace and QUIET!
(JEFF crosses to dummy and picks it up, he gives one end to SANDY and both boys race around the room like an ambulance. They dump the dummy on the bed.)

SANDY: *(Out of the fantasy)* Jeff, I'm going now.

JEFF: You can't; this is the best part!
(BEN and HELEN rise and cross to the bed. They kneel on either side of it. JEFF takes the two chairs and places them near the bed. JEFF and SANDY sit on the backs of the chairs with their feet on the seat, overlooking the scene. In this scene, everyone treats the dummy as JEFF.)

HELEN: Jeff, Jeff, this is your Mother.

BEN: Son, we're right here.

SANDY: He seems to be in a coma.

JEFF: But he can still hear you.

BEN: You've got to get well, son.

SANDY: So, he gets well and everybody lives happily ever...
(SANDY starts off the chair, JEFF pulls him back.)

JEFF: Not yet.

BEN: How do you feel son?

HELEN: Where does it hurt?

BEN: Can you hear us?

SANDY: No, he can't! His ears are filled with wax!

JEFF: Yes, he can! Go on!

HELEN: We promise things will change.

BEN: We'll do anything.

SANDY: Get him some soup! Get him a comic book!

JEFF: No, don't. Keep talking.

BEN: From now on, we'll be a family again.

JEFF: He's starting to come 'round.

SANDY: Still looks out of it to me.

HELEN: We'll all stay together, right here, we promise.

JEFF: He's definitely beginning to come 'round.

HELEN: If only we'd listened to each other.

BEN: If only we'd taken more time. If only your Mother had paid more attention.

HELEN: If only your Father had been home more.

SANDY: There they go again.

JEFF: Hey, he's back in a coma!

BEN: *(To HELEN)* This is all your fault, you know.

HELEN: My fault? Why is it always my fault?

JEFF: Will you look at your son?

HELEN: At least I tried, I helped him with his model and that's more than I can say for you.

BEN: Oh yeah, well, I would have helped him, if you'd just given me a chance!

JEFF: He's dying!

HELEN: I can't talk to you, you're impossible!

BEN: I'm impossible? You're impossible!
(They both storm off and exit through their posters. JEFF and SANDY sit, looking at the patient for a long beat. SANDY jumps down and begins to march around the bed singing the FUNERAL MARCH.)

SANDY: Dum dum dee dum, Dum dee dum dee dum dum dum.

JEFF: Cut it out, Sandy. *(The phone rings. SANDY continues. The phone rings again. JEFF makes no move to answer it. The phone rings again.)*

SANDY: Jeeze, Jeff, doesn't anyone around here ever answer the phone? *(SANDY answers the phone.)* Hello? Stuarts' residence. . . Oh, hi, Mom.. . Yeah, this is me... Obviously, I'm still here if I answered the phone ... No, what time is it? ... Aw, do I have to? ... Yeah, I know... Yeah, I know... Yeah, I know... Okay, right away... Yeah, I know! Bye. *(SANDY hangs up and turns to JEFF)* I gotta go. I have an appointment with the orthodontist.

JEFF: Orthodontist?

SANDY: I hate it when my Mom makes me dentist appointments during vacations. I don't even get to get out of school.

JEFF: Do you have to go?

SANDY: Yeah.

JEFF: Can't you tell her you're sick or something?

SANDY: Then she'd just make me come home and go to bed.

JEFF: Can't you tell her I'm sick?

SANDY: She'd be afraid I'd catch it, she'd still make me come home.

JEFF: Can I come with you?

SANDY: To the orthodontist?

JEFF: Sandy, I need you to stay with me, just five more minutes.

SANDY: What good would it do? Jeff, you can't change anything by not talking to them. *(JEFF turns away.)* Things will be better when it's over.

JEFF: When what's over?

SANDY: After you've talked to them.

JEFF: Are you sure?

SANDY: No. Bye, Jeff. See you tomorrow.

JEFF: Yeah.

SANDY: *(On his way out)* Hey, take it easy.

JEFF: Okay. *(SANDY exits, JEFF turns away. JEFF sees the dummy and runs after him.)* Hey, Sandy, just a minute, you forgot... *(JEFF exits through the small door, but he returns immediately dragging the dummy behind him.)* Damn! *(JEFF dumps the dummy on the floor and looks at the large door, he paces back and forth across the room. On each pass, he kicks the dummy out of the way.)* Can't feel that, can you? *(He continues to kick the dummy.)* Or that! Or that! You can't feel anything! *(After one last savage kick, JEFF picks the dummy up in his arms and hugs it tightly. He places it tenderly on the bed. JEFF crosses to the large door. He opens it and stands in the doorway.)* What are you doing?

BEN'S VOICE: Packing.

JEFF: Another business trip?

BEN'S VOICE: Not this time, son. *(JEFF turns away and steps back into his room.)* Jeff, come back in here.

JEFF: I don't want to!

BEN's VOICE: I'll get your Mother. She's making coffee. You wait right there. *(JEFF stands near the door for a moment and then bolts into his parents' room. He returns to his room immediately with a suitcase.)* Hey, what are you doing? *(BEN enters and faces JEFF. JEFF holds the suitcase defiantly.)*

JEFF: Why are you packing?

BEN: I've got to get out of here and let things settle down for a while.
 (JEFF drops the case on the floor, falls to his knees and begins pulling articles of clothing out of the case.)

JEFF: You can't take these, they're dirty. I'll wash them for you! *(JEFF throws a handfull of clothing on the floor.)*

BEN: Hey!

JEFF: Can't take these, they've got holes in them.

BEN: What are you doing?

JEFF: Can't take these, they're too old. Just rags! Can't take rags!

BEN: Easy, Jeff.
(JEFF rises with the case and dumps the rest on the floor.)

JEFF: You can't take them! They belong here! *(JEFF hurls the empty suitcase to the ground.)*

BEN: For God's sake, Jeff!

JEFF: You can't leave! We've got to all stay here, together! *(BEN reaches out to JEFF.)*

BEN: Let me talk to you!
(JEFF pulls away viciously.)

JEFF: Don't touch me!

BEN: Oh, God, Jeff! *(BEN is near tears.)*

JEFF: And don't you DARE cry!

BEN: Please, try to understand.

JEFF: Understand what?

BEN: Your Mother and I fight all the time, you must have heard us!

JEFF: I just turn up the T.V. and I don't hear anything.

BEN: That doesn't mean it isn't happening.

JEFF: I don't have to hear this! *(JEFF starts to try to leave. BEN stops him.)*

BEN: Yes, you do! Now, sit down. *(BEN sits him on the bed.)* It's happening and it has been happening for months, and you know it!

JEFF: No, I don't!

BEN: Yes, you do! There hasn't been peace or quiet or comfort in this house for a long time, and you know that, too.

JEFF: How do you know what I know?

(HELEN enters and stands in the doorway, with two coffee cups.)

HELEN: Jeff, honey, please listen to us.

JEFF: Mom, ask him not to go!
(BEN and HELEN look at each other.)

BEN: Jeff, about a week ago, I moved into a hotel, just temporarily, until I could find an apartment.

JEFF: Is that where you've been sleeping?

BEN: Yes.

HELEN: *(Astonished)* You knew?

JEFF: I've seen you go every night.

BEN: *(To HELEN)* I knew we shouldn't have done it this way, we should have told him when I first left.

HELEN: Ben...

JEFF: But every morning you'd be back for breakfast.

BEN: *(To HELEN)* I told you this wouldn't work.

HELEN: Alright, Ben! *(To JEFF)* Why didn't you say something?

JEFF: Why didn't you?

HELEN: I still hoped that we could work things out. We were seeing a counselor and I thought if we could just solve some of the...

JEFF: I can help!

HELEN: No, Jeff there's nothing you can do.

JEFF: I can help around the house more. I can be quieter. I can stay out of the way more.

HELEN: You are not responsible for this in any way.

JEFF: From now on, I'll clean up my room, I won't play the T.V. loud or the stereo...

HELEN: Jeff...

JEFF: Just tell me what I did wrong and I'll fix it; I will!

BEN: Jeff, you are the one really good thing in our lives. You were never the problem.

JEFF: So, why are you doing this?

HELEN: It's complicated ... there are so many reasons.

JEFF: Like what?

HELEN: Things we thought we wanted when we got married, just don't seem to be the things we want now.

JEFF: What things?

BEN: Jeff, I need ... want, your Mother to be the kind of wife she just can't be to me anymore. And she wants ... needs things from me that I just can't give her. We can't keep living this way, Jeff!

JEFF: Because you fight? So what?

HELEN: It isn't only the fighting, Jeff.

JEFF: So, just stop! Stop fighting! Everything would be okay if you'd just ...

BEN: It's why we fight.

JEFF: *(Very belligerent.)* Oh, yeah? Why?

BEN: *(Blurts it out)* We just don't love each other anymore. *(HELEN is shaken by this.)*

HELEN: Ben.

BEN: *(Realizing it himself for the first time.)* That's it, isn't it, Helen?

HELEN: I have never heard you say that before.

BEN: That's what's really wrong, isn't it?

HELEN: If we could just solve some of the problems.

BEN: *(Simply)* Helen, do you love me?

HELEN: I don't think we should talk about that here.

BEN: Do you love me?

HELEN: There are things I love about you.

BEN: That's not what I ...

HELEN: I know what you asked me.

BEN: And?

HELEN: *(Inaudible)* No.

BEN: Helen?

JEFF: Mom?

HELEN: No. *(There is a long pause.)*

JEFF: Will you get a divorce?

HELEN: *(After a beat)* Probably.

JEFF: And if I don't want you to?

BEN: I'm sorry, Jeff.

JEFF: But you're getting a divorce.

BEN: Not from you. *(BEN tries to touch JEFF who pulls away.)* This day, Jeff, this day is the hardest. Things will be better for all of us when this day is over.

JEFF: And then what happens to me?

HELEN: You'll stay here with me for now and then we'll. . .

JEFF: I mean, who do I live with? Will I have to go to Portland? What if I don't want to go? Will I have to leave all my friends?

BEN: We'll settle all that later.

JEFF: How do I know you aren't lying to me again?

BEN: *(Very firmly)* Just a minute, Jeff, we may not have told you everything that was going on, but we never meant to lie to you.

HELEN: And when I tried to talk to you, you wouldn't listen. You just turned away and tuned me out.

JEFF: From now on, will you tell me things?

BEN: Yes.

HELEN: From now, will you listen?

JEFF: *(Softly)* I'll try.

BEN: We've got two whole months to figure this Portland thing out, so let's just take it a step at a time. Okay?

JEFF: Do I have a choice?

BEN: Come on, Jeff. I think you'll like my apartment. It has a room for you, and an elevator, and a pool...

JEFF: Can I have a dog?
(Both BEN and HELEN laugh.)

BEN: We'll see.

JEFF: Will you ever decide to get back together again?
(They are caught off guard and hesitate.)

BEN: I don't think so.

JEFF: Mom?

HELEN: No. *(There is an awkward pause.)*

BEN: Well, if I'm going to get moved in to the apartment, I'd better get with it. I still have to check out of the hotel and.... *(He checks his watch.)* I'll come back for this stuff, Helen, okay?
(HELEN nods. BEN takes a card out of his pocket and writes on it.)

BEN: Jeff, let me write down the address of the apartment for you. Come see me anytime. I've got a phone, so just call and I'll come for you.

JEFF: *(Turns away from him.)* I can take the bus.

BEN: Anytime, Jeff, I'll come for you anytime... *(No response from*

JEFF.) I'll call you. *(He stands there for a moment, uncertain.)* Jeff? *(He holds out his arms, JEFF crosses to him and hugs him. Before the hug is really completed, JEFF pulls away.) (BEN looks at Helen, she is looking away.)* Helen? ... Take care. *(He starts out.)*

HELEN: You too. *(BEN exits.)*
(We hear BEN'S footsteps disappearing. A final door shuts off stage and the sound shudders through HELEN'S body.)

HELEN: *(After a beat to compose herself)* You okay?

JEFF: *(Shrugs)* You?

HELEN: Lousy.

JEFF: Me, too.

HELEN: Well, at least we're lousy together.

JEFF: Yeah. *(After a beat)* I hate this.

HELEN: I know. I hate it with you. *(JEFF turns to her and looks away. HELEN moves toward him slightly and speaks from her own need for comfort as much as his.)* Jeff, what do you do when you feel rotten? What do you do when you're really depressed?

JEFF: I don't know. . Nothing... Sometimes I take a walk and just look around for something I like. Something like a leaf or a piece of glass or something, and I just look at it for a while.

HELEN: *(This is a risky question for her.)* Want to take a walk?

JEFF: *(His voice says 'yes', his body says 'no'.)* Okay.

HELEN: I'll get the house key. *(HELEN exits to her room. JEFF crosses to the desk and picks up the card, he looks at it and puts the card in his pocket. He gathers up BEN'S clothes, and puts them in the suitcase. HELEN enters and stands in the doorway.)*

JEFF: After we get back, I'll take these over to Dad's. *(JEFF indicates the dummy.)* And then I'll take this over to Sandy's.

HELEN: Okay.

JEFF: Let's go, Mom. *(He holds out his hand to her. She takes it and they exit. Lights dim to black.)*

Curtain

Production Notes

Off-stage Argument
I have deliberately not written specific dialogue for the off stage argument. In an earlier draft I did try to sketch it out, but I felt it tended to limit and constrain the actors, and sounded artificial.

It is my intention that the argument should be created improvisationally by the actors and the director.

Some guidelines might be helpful:
It should be a real argument, and not random words or sounds.
The actors should decide what specific circumstances have led Ben and Helen to this particular moment.
The dynamics of the argument must be modulated to work with the primary action on stage. Off-stage sounds must never overwhelm what is happening on stage, but should underscore action.
When Ben and Helen enter a scene on stage in 'reality' they bring some of their previous offstage emotions with them. When they enter a scene in 'fantasy' they are primarily projections of Jeff's thoughts, fears, hopes, and feelings.

Treatment of the Fantasies
Fantasies are grounded in Jeff's needs in real life. It is this relevance to reality, rather than a departure from the real world, that gives these scenes their power.

Every director will interpret this in a different way, and will make his or her own stylistic choices. Light and sound can be important elements in introducing and underscoring these scenes. Fantasies must move the dramatic action of the play forward, rather than divert it.

A Final Note
The words and actions of this play provide all the essentials for production; but much of the depth and intensity of this script must be found between the lines, in subtext, and in silence. I urge you to be bold in your emotional choices, to be clear and specific with the development of relationships, and to bring the same emotional intensity to the words of the text and the thoughts and to feelings which remain unspoken.